YO-CXM-153

The publisher and author have made every effort to ensure the complete accuracy and currency of all information contained within the pages of *5 Chart Patterns: For Consistent Profits*, however, neither the author nor the publisher can accept any responsibility for any loss or inconvenience sustained by any reader as a result of the information or advice provided in this book. This publication is designed to provide general information regarding the subject matter covered; the information, ideas, and suggestions in this book are not intended to be financial or legal advice. Laws and practices often vary from region to region, and are subject to change. In addition to this, the financial markets are often highly speculative in nature, resulting in either tremendous loss or profit for the investor. Neither the author nor the publisher of this book is responsible for your use/misuse of the information presented in this book. By reading this book you agree to assume all risk from your investing activities. Do not embark on any financial venture without first consulting a licensed financial adviser in your jurisdiction. All trademarks used herein are the property of their respective owners. The use of any trademark in this text does not vest in the author or publisher any trademark ownership rights in such trademarks, nor does the use of such trademarks imply any affiliation with or endorsement of this book by such owners. Any institutions or organizations mentioned are purely anecdotal, and not an endorsement of that organization's services. Because of the dynamic nature of the internet, any web addresses or links outlined in this book may have changed since publication and may no longer be valid. All rights reserved. No part of this publication may be reproduced, stored in a retrieval system, or transmitted in any form or by any means, electronic, mechanical, photocopying, recording or otherwise, without the prior written permission of the author except for the quotation of brief passages in reviews. Enquiries concerning reproduction outside the scope of the above, or to learn about other titles written by the author should be sent to the author directly https://ca/linkedin.com/in/ashbeebakht

ISBN-13: 978-1514862452
ISBN-10: 151486245X

5 CHART PATTERNS: FOR CONSISTENT PROFITS

Table of Contents

The purpose of this book is to familiarize you with five extremely powerful chart patterns that will help you to increase your odds of success when trading the financial markets regardless of you are trading stocks, forex, etc. Trading is an extremely difficult profession that requires hard work and dedication in order to master. The chart patterns outlined in this book are a distillation from my own experiences trading the financial markets.

My first recommendation to you is to carefully paper trade a few stocks using one chart pattern at a time until you fully understand the pattern and become profitable, this will dramatically increase your odds of success with the material covered in this book.

When you feel that as a trader you are sufficiently proficient enough to correctly identify signals, and yield more winning trades without getting stopped out, move on to the next pattern.

Significantly Increase The Odds In Your Favour

As a trader you need to understand why it is that you enter a particular position, what is your own specific reason for position entry, the answer can't be "it looks like it's going up". You can't put down money based on a gut feeling; you have to be motivated by a technical reason found in the chart that you are observing. Another factor that will influence your trading is volume. The average daily volume of a stock that you choose to trade should be at minimum 1M shares.

Be very cautious when risking your equity, make sure you have spent sufficient time paper trading, otherwise you will pay a lot of money in market tuition…and that can be quite costly.

Something else that will have to be considered is your personal workstation. Keep your work area clean, and uncluttered. A messy desktop will not allow you to think clearly, and will prove to be distracting. You will need a good monitor setup (2-3 monitors minimum) so that you have ample real estate to view charts, level 2, etc. You will also require high-speed Internet connection and a good direct access broker.

This is a serious profession based on mathematics and market psychology, so act professional. If you trade with a budget day trading casino mentality, you will quickly gamble away your entire account.

A Few Words About Charts

It took me a few months of experimenting to find my personal g-spot for my own chart setup. I'm going to offer up some tips on how you can best manage your own charting.

a) Keep it simple, and uncluttered. Have only the essential information displayed because you will spend a lot of time just waiting for a healthy setup to present itself. If you have a complex window to look at with a lot of flashing colours and numbers, you will only get eyestrain.

b) To reiterate on the first point, don't have too many technical indicators on your charts, especially indicators that conflict signals.

c) Have at least one broad market chart and one sector chart, are they making new highs today compared to yesterday? It is important to gauge the market relative to the previous trading day's range.

d) Have a time and sales window for your stock, is there a buy or sell pressure?

When reading your Level 2 window use it primarily for order routing only. You can't always base a trading decision on what information you see there, because there is a lot of bluffing and intentional manipulation that happens in Level 2. You need to focus on the big picture of the market first and foremost, is it a red or green day? Is it a volatile day or is it very choppy with deadly whipsaw like activity? After you have performed this initial diagnosis, then you can use the individual chart patterns to identify a profitable entry and exit point. A common beginner mistake is just jumping in and out whenever and where ever—an entry and exit point must be determined BEFORE you place the trade.

Now that we have that out of the way, let's get to charting!

1st Pattern: Double-Day High Breakout Just After Cup Pattern From The Open

Instructions :

1) Use a two-day chart with two-minute interval candlesticks as your primary chart. Your chart must display the volume data as well.

2) Perform a scan of your basket of potential trade stocks, and search for a stock that is getting ready to make a move above yesterday's high. For this type of play, resist purchasing in the "range" of yesterday's moves. Professional money flows in and out of a stock when it has gone over the previous day's high, or under the previous day's lows.

3) This type of trade takes on average 5-15mins to execute round trip.

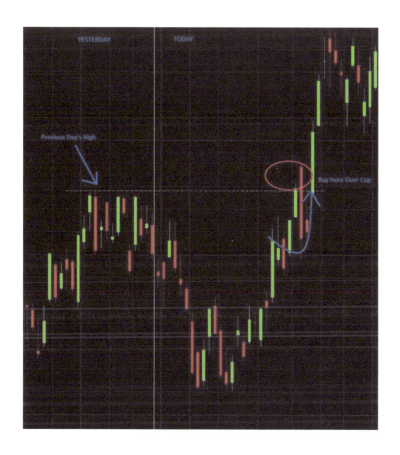

In the chart pictured on the previous page you can see the entry point would be above yesterday's high, and to play it safe you would wait for at least one candle to close to completion above yesterday's high. Another thing to consider is that it is useful to know your stock's average daily trading range, and resist the temptation to purchase if the stock is ¾ of the way into its daily range.

2nd Pattern: Double-Day Low Breakdown Short

This pattern is essentially the inverse of the 1st pattern that we explored in this book. In this scenario we scan for stocks that are cupping down from yesterday's low.

Instructions:

1) Just like with the 1st pattern utilize a two-minute candlestick chart, and scan for a stock that is dipping below yesterday's low.
2) The timeframe of this play can be longer than the 1st pattern.

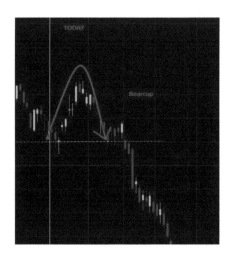

As with the 1st pattern to play it on the safe side you will wait until at least one complete candle breaks under the line of support set by the previous day's low. Know and understand your particular stock's daily trading range, and don't enter late. Use the time and sales data to monitor buy/sell pressure.

3rd Pattern: Long Pivot Fibonacci Bounce From Previous Daily Low

Breakouts can easily become your most profitable trades, and should constitute at least 80% of your plays on the markets. The following scenario is ideal to make money on a bounce play from a two-day daily chart.

Instructions:

1) In this scenario scan for a quick multipoint descent from yesterday's low, followed by a cup pattern reversal bounce. You must ensure that there is a cup pattern, otherwise you are just speculating on the bottom and could be catching a falling knife.
2) Scan for significant strength in the volume to carry the move.
3) Use the Fibonacci retracement feature of your charting package for your exit at 38% of the drop.

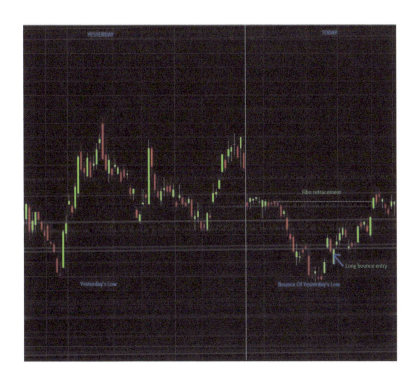

Bounce plays are always a bit tricky and can be risky, so make sure to paper trade this scenario a few times before you trade it live. Confirm the play with data from the time and sales window, and keep an eye out for the doji candlestick to signal a reversal. A full explanation of the different candlestick patterns is beyond the scope of this book.

4ᵗʰ Pattern: Gap Open Reversal And Gap Fills

This is an easy play so make sure to profit whenever you find this type of pattern.

Instructions:

1) Scan for a stock that has gapped at least 15% in the premarket. You will need a data package from your broker to view this sort of information.
2) The stock has to gap at least 15% outside of yesterday's range. Set your entry point above the current gap up/down for both the continuation and reversal plays on the open.
3) Wait until the market has opened and some form of direction is established before entering a position. Be on the look out for a large gap down recovery that is building a new cup formation high over yesterday's high, or get ready to short a premarket gap up on a bear cup pattern that is breaking down below the yesterday's premarket low.

5ᵗʰ Pattern: Double Top Chart Pattern

The double top reversal pattern is a bearish pattern. What you need is an early prior trend that is positive in order for it to be a double top.

Instructions:

1) The stock must be moving upwards in a positive trend.
2) The stock will reach a highest point at which traders don't feel that the stock price should rise further (Line of Resistance), and this will cause the stock to start to drop in price.
3) After dropping the stock will hit the "Line of Support", and then start to trend back up. The stock will then again make a second point of contact at the Line of resistance. At this second point the stock will be forced to reverse because of lack momentum and market sentiment. Just remember "M for murder", as you will see the letter "M" on your chart.
4) If the stock then drops below the Line of Support a second time, you can safely enter a short position.

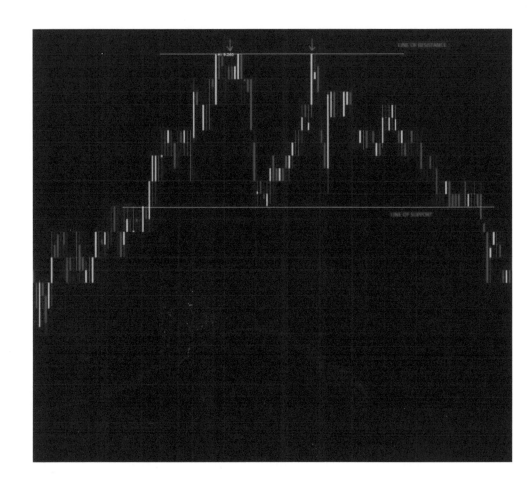

These five chart patterns have proved to be extremely profitable for my own personal trades, with sufficient practice, they will also prove to be very lucrative for your own account. Good luck, and happy trading!

ISBN-13: 978-1514862452
ISBN-10: 151486245X

CPSIA information can be obtained
at www.ICGtesting.com
Printed in the USA
LVHW071545261021
701537LV00020B/2